D1545092

WELCOME TO I SPY Everything BOOK

Let's Begin!

I SPY with my little eye, an AEROPLANE

A is for Aeroplane!

Bubbles

Door

Chair

Shoe

Strawberry

Ruler

I SPY with my little eye, a BOOK

B is for Book!

Rabbit

House

Flower

Orange

Milk

Pencil

I SPY with my little eye, a **CUP**

C is for Cup!

Spider

Watch

Ball

Socks

Paper

Egg

I SPY with my little eye, a DUCK

D is for Duck!

Koala

Octopus

Water

Mermaid

Clock

Bee

I SPY with my little eye, a EAR

E

is for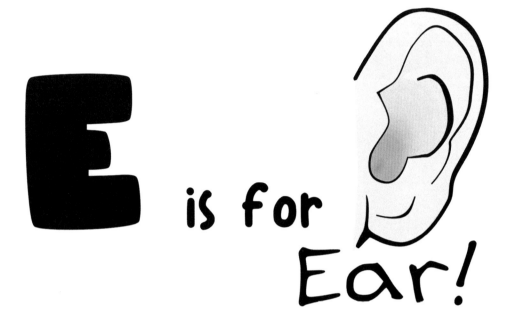

Ear!

Rocket

Bell

Table

Rabbit

Whale

Dog

I SPY with my little eye, a FAN

F is for Fan!

Tree

Ship

Mouth

Cloud

Banana

Car

I SPY with my little eye, GRAPES

G is for Grapes!

Candy

Eye

Bed

Moon

Hippopotamus

Bread

I SPY with my little eye, a **HAND**

H is for Hand!

Fire

Cake

Cap

Sun

Nest

Boat

I SPY with my little eye, ICE

 is for

Ice!

Nose

Top

Piano

Dress

Watermelon

Stars

I SPY with my little eye, JELLY

J is for Jelly!

Ice Cream

Box

Shirt

Foot

Sheep

Baby

I SPY with my little eye, a KITE

K is for Kite!

Cupboard

Train

Mushroom

Donut

Teeth

Penguin

I SPY with my little eye, a LEMON

L is for  Lemon!

Balloon

Rainbow

Glass

Ribbon

Hat

Straw

I SPY with my little eye, a MANGO

M is for Mango!

Lamp

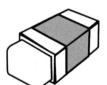

Eraser

Lightning

Grass

Unicorn

Corn

I SPY with my little eye, a NUT

N is for Nut!

Bus

Mirror

Starfish

Spaceship

Stone

Carrot

I SPY with my little eye, an ORANGE

is for Orange!

Guitar

Snowman

Television

Eggplant

Glasses

Spoon

I SPY with my little eye, a PIG

P is for  Pig!

Umbrella

Cookie

 Pear

Bowl

Curtain

Sausage

I SPY with my little eye, a QUILT

Q is for  Quilt!

Cactus

Glove

Snow

Teapot

Fork

Pumpkin

I SPY with my little eye, a RADISH

R is for Radish!

Shovel

Pail

Rain

Olive

Plate

Sandwich

I SPY with my little eye, a SQUIRREL

S is for Squirrel!

Ladder

Peach

Pants

Astronaut

Cucumber

Telephone

I SPY with my little eye, a TOMATO

T is for  Tomato!

Clown

Flower

Bicycle

Robot

Leaf

Ambulance

I SPY with my little eye, a UNIFORM

U

is for

Uniform!

Pan

Belt

Seashell

Kiwi

Fire Engine

Bag

I SPY with my little eye, a VAN

V is for Van!

Ladle

Broccoli

Hair

Scissors

Cheese

Apple

I SPY with my little eye, a WINDMILL

W is for Windmill!

Unicycle

Raspberry

Toothbrush

Onion

Helicopter

Papaya

I SPY with my little eye, a XYLOPHONE

X is for Xylophone!

Panda

Tree Trunk

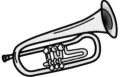

Trumpet

Cherry

Pineapple

Window

I SPY with my little eye, a YACHT

Y is for
Yacht!

Tornado

Hanger

Fries

Garlic

Potato

Capsicum

I SPY with my little eye, a ZUCCHINI

Z is for Zucchini!

Doctor

Drum

Eye

Sharpener

Beetroot

Coat

Made in United States
North Haven, CT
21 February 2023

32899120R00031